THE LITTLE BOOK OF BIG QUESTIONS:

A JOURNEY IN SELF DISCOVERY!

Sylvia High

Cover by Cheryl Denise Ward

THE LITTLE BOOK OF BIG QUESTIONS: A JOURNEY IN SELF DISCOVERY!

Library of Congress Cataloging -in-Publication Data

High, Sylvia, 1957-
The little book of big questions: a journey of self discovery! | Sylvia High.
p. cm.
ISBN: 0692381848
ISBN -13DIGIT: 9780692381847
1. Self help. 2. Personal growth. 1. Title.
LCCN: 2007927147 2007
0711

CIP

For speaking engagements, contact the author directly at:
Aiming High, Incorporated
(925) 634-0755

Printed in the United States of America.

Dedication

This book is dedicated to
my loving Mother,
whose unconditional love gave me the courage and the confidence to move through the world with joy and freedom.

To my husband,
my soul mate and best friend
who takes extraordinary care of my heart and nourish my spirit with love, joy, special moments and laughter. You have enriched my life in ways I can't begin to describe. I love you more each day.

To my family
who has loved me through thick and thin.
Through your love you have taught me how to be abundant with my love. Your humor has been the framework that has shaped our lives and added countless blessing and fond memories. Thoughts of each of you bring me warmth and joy daily. I am blessed to be apart of each of you, I am forever grateful to God for giving me you as a family.

Acknowledgements

Special thanks and gratitude to: my dear sweet sister Raynae, without her labor of love, time, brilliance, patience and support you would not be reading this book. Tina McCullom who took my handwritten scribble and typed the first version of a manuscript; my daughter Tiffany who did a round of editing and got out of her bed countless times to show me what to do on the computer. Maureen who took the time out of her busy schedule to share her expertise; Cynthia Henderson who spent many evenings creating a vision map, a list of things to do, inspiration to keep me going, love and laughter when I most needed to lighten up.

Julianna Hynes who read chapters, shared ideas, and gave me the gift of Cheryl Ward, an angel, publisher and friend. Cheryl Ward, for your incredible gift of seeing the finished product; the generosity of your gifts, time and talent and most of all your humor.

Amenita Rosebush for her brilliant insight and outstanding editing. Judi Henderson-Townsend and Dee Dee Rapp for articles on "How to get published." My niece Moria Taylor, and my sister, Inez Bentley, for your honest feedback, even when I didn't agree. My brother Tyron who said, "You can do it! You can go all the way! Don't stop!"

Robin Lynn, who believed I could master the conversations of possibility, even when I was not sure. Thanks for standing for me in the face of no evidence. To all of my Sister-friends, who have believed in me and all of my projects, the brilliant and the not so brilliant ones. Each of you know exactly who you are, we have traveled many miles and many years together. I will be forever grateful. Thanks from the depths of my heart.

Always aiming high with love,

Sylvia

Contents

The Journey

Self Discovery

Relationship Discovery

Creative Discovery

Spiritual Discovery

The Journey

The purpose of this book is to share a process I have used to keep stretching and growing in my personal and professional life; this tool has kept me appreciating life by using the power of self-reflection and self-examination. As you will see, each reflection is posed as a question. I do this because for years now, I have used the art of asking myself provocative and challenging questions to dig deeper into soul knowledge and find my own personal truth. Initially, I asked these questions quite by accident; however, after a breakthrough I had one day using questions to probe the mysteries of life; this process became a life strategy.

For many years, I went from job to job, quitting, getting fired, and then finding new jobs – only to have the same thing happen again. They were great jobs, with great pay, great people, excellent organizations, and outstanding perks and benefits; yet happiness and success always seemed to elude me. After six years of quitting, getting fired, and finding new jobs - only to have the same thing happen all over again - I decided to stop the insanity. I shall never forget the day. It was a cold and rainy Seattle afternoon. I was so-o-o-o tired of myself and the same old job saga. For years and years it was always the company's fault, the boss, the industry, or the unrealistic expectations that were placed on me, Blah, Blah… Blame, blame, blame, when in fact I was the one responsible. I was the only common denominator in this six year equation. Me - I was it, no one else. I had to reach a breaking point before I woke up. I grew so depressed, sad, tired and exhausted from crying my eyes out (you could have filled Lake Washington with my tears) that I had to make a change. I looked up from my state of despair and decided to ask myself why things were the way they were, why I was the way I was. And so I began to ask myself a series of provoking questions, and afterwards, I started to see new possibilities for myself that I hadn't seen when I was wallowing in unhappiness and self-pity. In other words, it wasn't until I stopped to inquire into myself and my experience of the world, as well as the ongoing issues in my life, that a light began to shine. The questions I posed however were not the normal questions like who was right and who was wrong, or what did I like and what didn't I like. All that had ever given me was the same old superficial answers, and they hadn't pulled me out of my depression. They were psychologically focused, inward focused, "me" focused. They did not have the ability to shed wisdom or add insight. My intuition told me that I had to go deeper and to look from a different perspective. How was I relating to the world? What attitudes did I hold and how did they influence the decisions I made? What happened in my past that was catching up to me today? What I saw was that I needed to ask committed, action-related questions that provoked me to see what I was actually doing that was sabotaging my life. They required me to focus outward and take action, not just sit around like a potted plant without moving; rehashing the same old poor me inward focused questions.

I am sure you have an area in your life with this type of theme or reoccurring patterns. It may be a pattern of bad relationships and poor choices in mates, it might be financial challenges, it could be issues with your weight or some form of addictions. Rehashing and asking inward focused questions fuels reoccurring patterns. Rehashing does not give access to new possibilities or new choices. The series of questions that I came up with that changed my life are presented here in this book. They shifted my perspective and they will shift yours too. You must commit to answering them honestly. They represented the beginning of a seismic shift in how I conducted my life, which led me to breaking free from being a victim to being accountable, from no possibility to possibility, from it's too late to it's never too late. I learned to live an empowered life with clear intention and personal commitment.

Of course, it takes some discipline to make changes like these. Many of you reading the word discipline will think, "Oh no, that means it's going to be hard." Well yes, it can be. But think of how much harder it is to be enslaved by our shortcomings and negative attitude. Think of it this way: discipline gives us freedom. On the other hand, I also subscribe to spontaneity and moving through life with ease. How does this balance with discipline? Even when you are requiring yourself to face something difficult, to overcome a challenge you would rather shrink from, you can always find the grace to treat yourself with compassion and dignity. This determines how we will experience the whole process of inquiry: with joy, excitement, loving-kindness, or dread. The first option will allow you to move effortlessly through the process. I am never cavalier. I take it very seriously, yet I never forget to let joy shine down.

I have also found that I cannot afford to drop the ball. It is imperative to take the time to examine my thoughts, emotions, and actions on a regular basis if I want to grow and bloom into my best self, if I want to learn more about my life and its process. Through this process of consistent self-examination, I have been blessed. I have created a thriving training and consulting business that has helped thousands of people change their lives. I use my gifts to coach both people and organizations to breakthrough their limitations and reach their goals, whether they be personal or professional. At this point in my journey, I have a meaningful and exciting marriage, a strong spiritual life, an intimate relationship with God, rewarding relationships with friends and family, and a life that is balanced and fulfilled. It may not be perfect, but it is deeply satisfying and every day is a rich new experience. It is my firm commitment to be a teacher as well as a student of life until I die. I find it valuable beyond measure when we share our wisdom and when we are open to new wisdom.

Wherever you are in life, remember: it's never too late to begin again. I am living proof that this process can work. So start by asking yourself provocative questions:

What are you pretending not to know?
What do you really want?
What matters to you?
What are your gifts and talents?
What brings you joy?

ONE

Self Discovery

ONE

Self Discovery

Discovery is a very powerful thing. Just think about how different this world would be without it. If the great discoverers did not stop and question the way things were, if they did not challenge the status quo, if they did not ask what was possible, how different would this world be? There would be no airplanes, no electricity, no running water, no computers, no cell phones, and no cure for many diseases. We would not enjoy the Golden Gate Bridge, the Eiffel Tower, the Ancient Ruins, or the Pyramids. Each one of these discoveries has added enormous value and advancement to our planet. They have improved the way we live, the way we communicate and in some cases, how long we can live. While these discoveries are great, the journey of life has taught me the most powerful discovery of ALL is SELF-DISCOVERY!

Every time we discover one new thing about ourselves, there is more of us available to us. The more of you that is available to you, the more empowered you are to leverage yourself with yourself and others. The more we are able to leverage *ourselves* with ourselves and with others, the more empowered we become to make profound shifts in our lives and in the world. It is from this place that we are able to create extraordinary futures, futures that weren't going to happen automatically. It is through the journey of self discovery that we gain new insights about who we are, increase our confidence, our courage, renew our passion, reflect on our past, tell the truth about what is and powerfully declare what shall be, based on our own passion, beliefs, and values. When we take the time to self-discover, we begin to be very intentional about the way we live, what we do with our time and who we spend our time with, creating necessary boundaries and strategies to insure our wholeness. We do not run the risk of falling asleep in our lives and missing what matters most to us, as unique and special gifts to the planet. We are creating for ourselves a life that is richer and driven by our own core values, desires, and dreams. Self-discovery forces us not to get on automatic pilot. It pushes us past any form of survival and keeps us acutely aware of what is important and why it is important. Self-discovery does not automatically happen. It only happens when we are willing to ask ourselves powerful, thought provoking questions; questions that reveal that which is not transparent to us at the time. It is through this process of revealing underlying assumptions and beliefs that were hidden that we are able to access more of who we are capable of being, and what we are capable of feeling and experiencing in the world. As long as our beliefs are hidden from us, we don't have the beliefs they have us and we lack the choices and possibilities that comes with expansion of self through self-discovery.

One of the most significant and challenging things about children is that they are full of questions. Even when we give them answers, more often than not, they have questions about the answer. They are absolutely in awe of life and the process. However, as adults we get answers about different aspects of our lives and who we are and we proceed to operate out of these set answers, never stopping to reflect, examine, or challenge these answers no matter how archaic or inapplicable the answers may be. We do not take into account how different we are or how we have changed. We somehow fail to examine these perspectives that so profoundly shape the way we operate in our lives, which in turn affects every component of our lives and the results we are creating for ourselves.

This reminds me of a story I once heard about a little girl. The little girl was watching her mother make Christmas dinner. Her mother was preparing a ham. She seasoned it with cloves and pineapples, and then cut off both ends of the ham before placing it in the pan and into the oven. Curious, the little girl asked, "Mother, why did you cut the ends off the ham before placing it in the pan?" The mother replied, "Honey, that's the way my mother always cooked her ham." So in a child's curious way the little girl proceeded to the living room and asked her grandmother, "Grandmother, why do you cut the ends off the ham?" "Honey, that's the way my mother always cooked her ham." Still not satisfied, the little girl went to her great-grandmother and asked, "Great-grandmother, why do you cut the ends off the ham?" Her great-grandmother replied, "Honey, because I did not have a pan big enough for the ham to fit in and I could not afford to buy a new one."

So you see it pays to ask questions. Though this may be a simple story, my questions to you are: Where in your life are you not asking questions? What old premises, ideas, or information are you using to guide your life that are no longer valid, useful, or in some cases, ineffective? What old ideas or beliefs about yourself are you still using that are no longer accurate given your accomplishments, life experiences, values, and wisdom? When was the last time you stopped to question the way you see things and question the premises these ideas were built upon? Maybe you are operating from some old premise like the ladies baking the ham. I have no idea what limiting or dated beliefs you have, but what I do know is the moment we stop asking questions, it is at that precise moment that we stop growing.

The more I discover about myself (and you about yourself), the more doors and possibilities will open in our lives. When we are willing to be in an inquiry state versus " I know I have the answer" we are able to broaden our paradigm and perspectives. Every time you open up and ask questions and discover new things about yourself, your personal comfort zone expands. Which in turns gives you a tremendous leap forward and who you become in that moment is someone greater and wiser.

So, I invite you to join me on this journey of inquiry and

exploration. Come see what you may discover and whom you may meet along the way – perhaps a wiser you. Perhaps you may rediscover a childhood or perhaps you will invent a new you.

Take the time to reflect, ponder, challenge, and examine yourself, your perspectives, and what drives these perspectives. What are these perspectives built on? Where did they come from? Do they align with who you are now and what you value now? There is power in opening up and taking a good honest look no matter where you are in life – at the starting of something new and exciting, at a cross road, or in a place of contentment or despair. It is powerful and empowering when we recognize and honor what is true for ourselves and what is the truth even when the truth is tough to face.

It is being intentional about your life. It is you happening to your life instead of your life happening to you. It is "Living by design." It is inventing an extraordinary future that wasn't going to happen automatically. What does this mean? It means taking yourself on and pushing past the tough spots, risking in spite of fears. It means going too far in order to know how far you can go. It also means going on when the world says it can not be done and you are not the one. It means starting something new when statistics say you are too old, too young, or not smart enough. It means getting past your history and limiting beliefs that you and others have used to define you. For example: "You are shy," "You are a procrastinator," "You are not creative," "You are not good with money." It means challenging these beliefs and premises and engaging with them as just that: premises and not facts. It means when life is fine, work is fine, kids are fine, family is fine; yet you know there is more and you challenge yourself to the more. It means engaging fully and purposefully with yourself, your dreams, and the rest of the world each and every day. It means watching the attitude you bring to each morning and each situation, for it is these moments that make up our lives.

Be sure to do the work and journal the process as you become more and more of who you are. Capture your insights, your "aha's", your feelings of anger, fear, joy, and excitement. Consider working with a buddy or perhaps having conversation groups that meet once a month. There is enormous power in purposeful and thought provoking dialogue. Journal a question each day. Be sure to do the Reflection Check-In Questions. These are not exercises of the head, they are exercises from the heart, so be authentic and push for the truth. Start with whatever comes to mind. There is value in what seems to be random. I cannot tell you what you will discover. But I can promise a journey worth taking. So sit back, get a cup of tea, relax, and open up. Be a willing, eager, humble mind. Most of all question, question, and question some more……

Remember that the book is designed for self discovery, so take your time, go through the process, and journal the questions. Don't sensor your thoughts and feelings, let what comes up come out. In other words, keep it real and the truth will set you free. It will empower you and, more importantly, it will reveal *you* to you.

In what ways are you stealing life from yourself?

?

What type of things do you do to increase your experience of life? (Your "aha's", your feelings of anger, fear, joy, etc.)

What talents, gifts, and/or strengths do you refuse to own/ acknowledge? What would be different if you did?

Who have you decided you are? How is that working? (For example: I am powerful, creative, courageous, beautiful, smart, ugly, procrastinator, weak, less than others, etc.)

What negative, demeaning habits, thoughts, or ways of being (shy, whiny, angry, resentful, jealous) has a strong hold on you? Where did this come from?

Use fifteen words to describe yourself?

What is keeping you from being your ideal self?

When you squeeze and orange, orange juice comes out. If someone squeezes you what would come out? (For example, love joy, resentment, angry. Be honest)

TWO

Do What You Can

The great tennis player Arthur Ashe once said, "Do what you can, with what you have, where you are." One of the greatest problems for so many people is that they can't get started because they are unwilling to embrace where they are and what they have. Saying "If only …" and then being stuck in one place robs them of their joy. Never reaching their goals creates endless disappointment. When you spend so much time wishing things were different – wishing you had more money, wishing you had a bigger house, wishing you were smarter, wishing you were taller, wishing, wishing, wishing – you focus all your attention on what is missing, not on what is present. What do you have right now? What are your gifts? What are your strengths? What are your accomplishments? Once you realize what you really have, you can use these gifts to move on to the next level. You only have to ask yourself what do I need and who can help me get to the next level.

It is a funny thing about life. Whatever we focus on grows the most. Wherever we place our attention is where our power – or lack of it – will be. A man with no hair, for instance, might go into a job interview and be thinking obsessively about his missing hair and how un-masculine that makes him look. This robs him of his confidence. Another man who is bald barely gives it a thought., in fact he finds himself rather handsome with his bald head. So, where is your power? Is it on what you have and what you can do, or is it on what you cannot do? I suggest you follow the advice of Arthur Ashe: "Do what you can, with what you have, where you are." You might be surprised at what you will achieve when you focus on your possibilities, gifts, and talents. Shift your mind and become a member of the glass-is-half-full club; as the story goes, the members of this club have created lives above and beyond what they thought possible. So go ahead and take heed, be obedient, and do what the great Arthur Ashe requested: Do what you can, with what you have, where you are, and please don't be surprised by the masterpiece that you will create, which is called an extraordinary life. Called your own unique life, filled with joy, fulfillment, accomplishments, and pure satisfaction.

There is nothing more rewarding than embracing who we are and where we are and moving forward in spite of limiting perspectives of ourselves, limiting thoughts about our abilities, resources, and our station in life. It is when we can look at that robber called wishing and comparing in the face and say No, I beg your pardon, who I am is enough, what I have is enough; in fact, I am more than enough and there is nothing I cannot achieve, starting right here where I am, with what I have. This is the moment that I declare that who I am is all that is wanted and needed. The power available to us when we place our focus on what we have is limitless.

What is the ideal you? How is this person different from who you are now?

What dream do you desire that you are unconsciously waiting for someone to validate? Why are you waiting for validation and permission?

In what areas of your life do you feel like you are not enough? What do you need to do to change this?

What popular limiting beliefs and ideas have you heard from others that you have adopted as your own? How are these things shaping or impacting your life? (Must work hard, can't trust people, can only count on yourself, etc.)

What part of yourself have you lost that would be a joy to recover?

What in your life do you need to say "no" to, but have been unwilling? What is the price you are paying? (What are you giving up?)

Name a time in your life when you knew better but did not do better? (Did not speak up, went along, and ignored or lied.) Why not, and what is it about this incident that makes it stand out in your mind?

What is the most dishonest thing you have ever done? How did you feel? What impact did this have on your life?

THREE

Do the Right Thing, Because It Is the Right Thing

When we do the right thing because it is the right thing (and we do it in the right way), great things will follow, starting with the building of our own character. I was struck by a sermon by Pastor Creflo Dollar entitled, "The Power of Doing the Right Thing Because It is the Right Thing, In the Right Way." Our overall quality of life rises when we live this way. It becomes a life filled with peace, pride, integrity, trust of others, and trust of ourselves. We develop strong character when we live our lives this way. Once we develop strong character we can be comfortable in all situations at all times. We are able to express ourselves as solid human beings with our feet planted firmly on the ground. We have nothing to hide, which gives us access to complete freedom. Freedom of full self-expression.

We all know that doing the right thing isn't always easy. It may mean taking an unpopular stand or being willing to stand alone because no one else had the courage to challenge the status quo. But the payoff is well worth the effort. When you can look yourself in the face every morning and know that you live and act with integrity, you have found something more precious than pearls. Of course, in life we have to compromise all the time, but somethings are too valuable to negotiate. At the top of the list of non-negotiables is our character. So we must protect it at all cost. At the end of life, this is all we really have to show for ourselves. No one lying on his/her death bed really cares how much money they made or how big their car was. They ultimately care whether they have peace with themselves and God and those they love. They care if they've lived an honest, good life.

Notice from above that we must not only do the right thing, but take care to do it in the right way, with the right attitude. If you keep these directives in the forefront of your mind, you will be a better person for it.

Remember, it is not just the big things that count. Excellence and integrity in the little things are just as important. Because character refers to your relationship with yourself, it matters just as much that you do the right thing when you're alone as well as when you are with others. There is no point in doing what's right only when others are watching. After all, your conscience is always watching. That's why it's important to have integrity even when you are the only one to witness it. This lends credibility with the person who counts the most - you. When we build credibility within our own self in little ways, then ourself believes us when we declare big dreams and big goals. The self aligns with appropriate actions to support the manifestation of these goals and dreams. It's when we don't do the right thing in the right way on a day-to-day basis that it takes a lot to convince the self that we are someone that is worthy of a rich full life, because we have not established ourselves with ourselves as someone with reliable and credible character...So you know what to do: The Right Thing Baby!

What is the most honest thing you have ever done? How did you feel? What impact did this act have on your life?

?

In what ways have you compromised yourself?

What, in your life, is stopping you? Why are you allowing this?

If life was made up of four quadrants:
1) Not playing at all (resigned, why bother?; it's always been this way; will always be this way, etc.)
2) Just playing (going along; taking life as it comes; whatever, whatever! etc.)
3) Playing not to lose (playing safe, concerned about image, approval, acceptance)
4) Playing to win (risking, vulnerable, going one hundred percent, passionate, etc.)
5) Which quadrant are you playing in? In what areas of life are you playing to win or not playing at all ?

Name the things you do that waste time. How do you avoid doing what needs to be done?

When was the last time you had a deep-belly, heartfelt, soul-moving laugh?

What racket, routines, or habits do you use to keep you from being your best self? (Procrastination, overwhelmed, over-commit, not committing.)

?

What winning formula do you use to call the best from yourself? (For example, do you work out, pray, meditate, or set goals?) How often are you doing these things?

FOUR

Your Vision Must Take Priority Over Your Circumstances

Some things in life are called "count-on-ables." They will be what they will be. Life will keep being life, the world will keep being the world, and people will keep being people. If you sit in a chair and wait for things to be perfect before you get out there and act, you will be sitting there for a long time. No matter what you do, there will always be joy and pain, sunshine and rain, good times and bad times, successes and disappointments. "Death and taxes," as someone once said, "you can never get away from them." This is just the nature of life. It's like a roller coaster. Sometimes it's on top and sometimes it will be on the bottom. This is what you can count on as long as you are alive. Life will always hand you challenges, no matter what you choose! The key is to keep your vision greater than life's challenges! This will keep you focused on moving forward instead of pulling you away every time something goes wrong.

Martin Luther King, Jr., Mother Theresa, and Ghandi are three people who faced enormous challenges. Most of the people they met probably told them that their goals were impossible. But they didn't listen because their vision was too big to forget or dismiss. It kept them going in the face of all difficulties. The world is a better place because their vision was greater than their circumstances and they held determination in the face of adversity. Remember, your vision is a priority and it will contribute to the fiber of your life and the fabric of the planet when it manifests. Therefore it is the vision that must stay senior and take our attention's priority, not the other way around. What happens for most of us is we start out strong and excited about our vision and dreams and then life starts to do it's thing and we begin to give all of life's incidentals and accidentals our priority and attention and the visions quickly begin to fade and sit on the shelves and collect dust and are soon forgotten. We must be like the Olympian that trains daily for the Olympics in the face of all of life's challenges, mishaps, and hardships; because despite these roadblocks, the Olympian pushes toward the prize until it is achieved and the vision is accomplished, until they win the gold, the silver, or the bronze. They know that no incident can be belabored, for the longer they belabor life's incidents and circumstances the farther away the vision moves, and if they don't return their focus quickly, soon the opportunity to accomplish the vision will no longer be within reach. This is not only the truth of the Olympian, it is also our truth, and it is therefore imperative that we always, always, without fail keep our vision senior to life's challenges, and our visions must take priority above all of life's ups and downs, joys and pains, sunshine and rain; for this is the gateway, the key to every vision manifestation.

What would be different if you approached each new challenge or situation with the attitude, "I have already made it," or "It's a done deal"?

What would you do if you weren't afraid? What are you afraid of?

What are your "Yeah, buts...."? What are these excuses costing you?

In what areas of your life are you playing the blame game? (It's someone else's fault, they did it to me; I'm not responsible.)

What is the single greatest thing about being a human being? What made you choose this particular aspect or characteristic and what does it say about you?

Who or what are you tolerating and doing nothing about? Why are you allowing this to continue?

What is the one thing about yourself you most want to change? Why?

What one habit or pattern would you like to shift or change? What would be different in your life?

What have you discovered so far?

How can these discoveries forward your life?

What actions will you commit to taking?

FIVE

Relationship Discovery

FIVE

Relationships

The relationships we develop – with our parents, siblings, children, spouses, friends, co-workers, and everyone we meet – shape us in ways we often cannot recognize and don't take the time to think about. In fact, these relationships shape our world. They shape our viewpoints and opinions, our likes and dislikes. They either build us up or tear us down. All of our beliefs and assumptions are based not only on the culture we live in, but also on our relationships. The beliefs that we are exposed to as children follow us into our adult lives. And these experiences of our youth make up our value system and beliefs today.

Childhood is a time when relationships have the greatest impact. A child is like a sponge, and it is easy to make an impression on him/her. The child is not particularly aware of what is taking place, that he/she is forming prejudices and seeing others through stereotypes. At some point, we must stop and examine ourselves in order to shake off the belief systems of the past that hold us back today and keep us from embracing new possibilities. As important as childhood experiences are, so are adult experiences, which carry their own weight and are also life defining. They, too, define and shape how we see the world. What's important is to be aware of how our experiences are affecting us. Otherwise, we will be condemned to acting out our beliefs. Someone once said, "An unexamined life is not worth living."

If you are afraid to examine yourself, to evaluate and determine what values and beliefs still fit and which ones should be discarded, then you are denying access to your authentic self, the power of choices, the gift of being present and the blessing of choosing what is real in the moment. Life is in the moment, not the past, not the future. Life only occurs in relationship. We as human beings only exist in relationship. How is your life unfolding and how do you show up for the world? What beliefs are determining how you experience the world and how the world experiences you?

What ongoing thoughts shape your reality?

What are you passionate about? Are you living this passion? If not, why not?

How would you show up if you were newly in love? (Vibrant, joyful, open, playful, delighted, etc.) What would be possible if you lived life this way?

How do you express your creativity? (Are you artistic, intuitive, have great style, an eye for beauty? Do you have a way with words? Are you intuitive with people, etc.) Look beyond the obvious. Are you using this creativity? If not, why not?

How do you spend most of your free time? What does this say about you?

What is your secret fantasy? What might this imply about you?

?

How do you recharge when you're running out of steam? How often do you do this?

What is your winning formula that calls the best from you?

SIX

Conversation

We are always one conversation away from transformation. Every time we speak to another person, we have an opportunity to speak possibility, to illumine and awaken. Even if it is a conversation about what kind of food we like, how we feel about a movie, our dreams, our heartfelt commitments, we may discover a whole new side of ourselves. We can open others to possibilities and we create new ones for ourselves as well.

Every dream is born in a conversation and every dream can be killed by a conversation. The Golden Gate Bridge was once a conversation. Flight was once a conversation. Electricity was once a conversation. The book you're holding in your hand was once a conversation. Too often we are careless about our language and forget the power and impact of the spoken word. Everywhere we go, our words affect the people around us. When we are cynical, negative, or dismissive, we can make others feel angry, ashamed, or despairing. There is an old saying, "Sticks and stones can break my bones, but words can never hurt me." This, quite simply, is a myth. We all know that words can cut deep and leave a bigger mark than a slap. We often heal much more quickly from a physical bruise than from an emotional one; a pointed insult sticks around inside our soul and damages our spirit. And what we choose to talk about shapes the world around us. It determines how we experience ourselves and how the world experiences us.

Think about it. If you talk about yourself like a loser, how will you feel about yourself? How will others see you? What would happen if you did the opposite?

The power of a conversation and our words is immense. Countries go to war over words. Language can cause feuds between families or between countries. Marriages and friendships break up because of it. You can crush your own dreams by negative self-talk. You can destroy the dreams of others by subtle ridicule and criticism or blatant judgment.

Take a moment to reflect on your life. Look at the past and at where you are now. What words do you choose to talk about yourself and to relate to the outside world? Are your words honest? Are they kind? Are your words empowering? Are they affirming? Do they build the spirit or break the spirit?

Remember, there is no such thing as a "throw-away line." Everything you say makes its mark, even if you think it is a casual statement. Our subconscious mind does not make any distinction between words that are haphazardly spoken and words that are spoken in earnest. Our mind takes it all in. So if you say something hastily in anger, use harsh and cruel words, you cannot take them back. They have made their impact! You can apologize and say you didn't mean it, but the injury has taken place. It will take that person some time to get over it – if ever. It is important to guard our language and our conversations with vigor because they are powerful forces. They can open doors for us, and can just as easily close them. We are always one conversation away from transformation. What are you transforming?

Name ten blessings that you are grateful for.

Name five self-imposed limiting beliefs. How are these impacting your life? (Too old, too fat, not smart enough, etc.)

What on-going thoughts do you have that are shaping your reality?

What are you empowered to shift in your life to more closely match your goal or vision?

Use ten words to describe your overall attitude. (Look at all aspects of your attitude.) What should you keep and what should you delete?

When you were born, what purpose showed up with you? Are you currently living out that purpose?

How do you approach the world? (From possibility, caution, fear, free reserved, playing it safe, risking, etc.) Use details (family, career, relationships, finances, etc.)

How do you approach a challenge? Is your first thought, "I can" or "I can't?" Is it solution focused or problem focused?

SEVEN

Inevitable vs Inventing

When a person has an "inevitable" attitude, it means they are resigned to the way things are and the way they've always been. That attitude pretty much dictates more of the same in the future: more of the same experiences, more of the same relationships, more of the same emotions, and ultimately, more of the same results. The very quality of life stays the same. When a person has an "inventing" attitude on the other hand, even though there is no evidence that the task can be done, even though she hasn't ever done it before, even though she is not an expert, and even though the world is not telling her to go for it, she is still willing to take a risk. Their own history may be screaming at them to play it safe, but they still muster up the courage to climb out on the skinny branch and reach for success. Her own past failures might warn her, "Why bother, you won't make it," but she'll go for it anyway. They will choose to do what everyone else said couldn't be done because in their heart and soul, they know differently. So by all means, proceed to create the extraordinary based on your own commitment and vision. What a difference a thought makes!

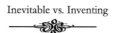

Think about it. If you talk about yourself like a loser, how will you feel about yourself? How will others see you? What would happen if you did the opposite?

What truly inspires you?

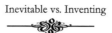

Given who you are, how can you serve the world? Are you doing it?

How can you rewrite your agreement with your reality and your interpretation of your life? (I was abandoned; my parents didn't love me; I can't trust men/women; this is the best I can do, be, have.) How would this alter your life?

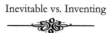

If you could impact the world in any way you wanted, how would you do it?

If you could ask God one question, what would you ask? Why this question?

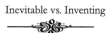

If you could ask Princess Diana one question, what would you ask her? Why this question?

If you could ask Martin Luther King Jr. one question,
What would you ask him? Why this question?

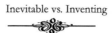

If you could ask Mother Theresa one question, what would you ask her? Why this question?

?

EIGHT

Living As Your Word

You and your word are one and the same. This means that what you say reflects who you are. It points directly to your character. You have to think of "giving your word" as "living your word." This means that you don't give it lightly, that there is a depth of understanding about the impact of giving your word. Whether you keep it after you give it defines you as a person, because giving and keeping your word is the equivalent of integrity.

Many of you will think that the point here is to turn yourself into a person that others can trust. Yes, but it's more than that. It's about being the person you can trust. It's important for other people to count on you, but can you count on yourself? When you say you'll do something, do you do it? Every time you give in on some small thing and take the easy way out rather than being true to your word, some part of you knows it cannot trust you. If you cannot be counted on for the small things, how can you trust yourself on the big things? If you say you're going to start your own business, for example, you have to begin by having a lot of faith in yourself or you won't have the confidence to overcome all the obstacles. What if you promised yourself all summer that you'd get up early and go jogging, and you just stopped doing it because you didn't feel like it? Did that failure to follow through inspire faith in yourself? Do you really believe, now, that you have the strength and the endurance to make a go of your own business, with all that it entails, if you couldn't keep a commitment to take a run every day?

Not keeping your word also has a deteriorating effect on relationships. It tears away at the fiber of the relationship. If you tell your mate that you will be home by seven and you are not there at seven, you rob that person of the trust he/she placed in you. If you do this all the time and with everyone, you rob all parties involved. People may not confront you about it and tell you that they feel betrayed or let down, but that doesn't mean it isn't true. The stories you make up, all your justifications, may sound good to you and for a while it will seem as if you're getting away with it. But justification plus excuses plus no results do not equal integrity and trust. If you think people are buying into your story, you are being sucked into an illusion. People are constantly making a decision about who you are and you are constantly making decisions about who you are as well. They are deciding how much you're going to be a part of their lives, if they can trust you, and if it is safe to freely connect with you. You are deciding if you can trust you and if it is safe to rely on you. Every single time you break your word you lose power, first with yourself and then with others. You lose the power of influence, credibility, and honor. When we break our word, this taints everything we do. It tints the lens through which others see us and the lens through which we see ourselves.

Even when we do follow through on our promises, people have a tendency to think it's an aberration. It takes a lot to win back trust and power once we've lost it because our words, in the past, haven't been backed by our actions. When the music and the words don't match, it's a bad song. If we don't live as our word, we rob ourselves of trust and integrity, and we rob our fellow beings of the opportunity to have faith in us. Perhaps our lack of integrity even chips away at others' ability to have faith in anyone. Not keeping our word is like a speck of sand in a gas tank. When these specks of sand happen too frequently and fill the gas tank, the engine stops running. So, be mindful of the specks.

If you could ask Jackie O one question, what would you ask her? Why this question?

If you could ask John F. Kennedy one question, what would you ask him? Why this question?

If you could ask Ghandi one question, what would you ask him? Why this question?

If you could spend the day with anyone in the world, who would it be? Why this person?

What would you be if you could be anything in the world? What is stopping you?

If you were the President, what law would you implement? Why?

If you were God, what one thing would you change? Why?

What would you do if money were not an issue? What is standing between you and more money?

NINE

Creative Discovery

NINE

Playing To Win

This is the question. The self-examination we must ask ourselves. Am I playing to win or am I playing not to lose? What is the difference? Well, there's a big difference, although not always obvious. Playing not to lose is wrapped in the need to look good, be accepted, and doing just enough to be above average. However, you know it's not your personal best. For example, it is having the wisdom to change a situation, but it would be uncomfortable to make waves. So instead of speaking up and sharing your wisdom, you opt not to rock the boat. It's settling for a good life versus an extraordinary life.

Playing to win is giving one hundred percent, one hundred percent of the time! When you're playing to win, you are alive, fully engaged, and living your purpose. It's a willingness to be vulnerable to your passion, to make mistakes and sometimes look bad. It can be humbling to follow your passion because at first you might not be very good at it. What if you decided at midlife to become a writer? Here you are struggling to be good at something when for the past twenty years you've been at the top of your game. Now you are a beginner. But being a writer is what you've always wanted. You make a lot of mistakes but it's okay. Because when you're playing to win, you're giving it all you've got, you're in the juice and the joy of life. In fact, when you're playing to win you will know. There will be no need for outside confirmation.

What would you do if time was not an issue? How can you make more time for yourself?

What would you do if you were more courageous? Why this? Why is this important to you?

What would you do differently with your life if you were completely honest with yourself?

Where would you go if you could go anywhere in the world? How would you spend the time there?

Name the top fifty things you want to do before you die.

Name your greatest strengths.

Name your greatest weakness.

What are you pretending not to know? (What are you stuffing, ignoring, avoiding, overlooking)

TEN

Clear Intention vs. "Efforting"

There's a big difference between "trying" and "efforting" to have something happen, and having clear intentions that something is going to happen. One approach, "efforting", is coming from the context of hoping, trying, wishing, "it's a nice idea," and "wouldn't it be great if?..." "Efforting" is easily swayed. All someone has to do is say, "you can't make it" and you're ready to give up. Or you come across one too many obstacles and you don't feel it's worth it. Or you begin to feel conflicted about whether you really want this at all. "Is it really worth all this trouble?" People who are "efforting" only want to keep going if it's easy, if it doesn't cost them too much. They believe that the power to achieve is outside of themselves, and therefore they allow outside forces to determine whether they reach their goals.

The context of trying is even worse. A good example is this: Try to pick up a pencil. No, don't actually pick it up. Just sit there and try to do it. Do you see what that feels like? It feels weak. The language of those with weak intentions is riddled with, "I'll try." That kind of language practically dooms them to failure because they're not at all clear that they are going to do it.

Clear intention is very different. It is rooted in the context: this shall happen, no matter what! "I don't care what it takes, how long it takes, how hard it is, who I have to ask for help, how it looks, how many times I fail, this shall happen!"

When our intentions are clear, we are unstoppable. It doesn't matter how many obstacles are thrown in our way. We intend to make it and we won't be stopped. If we fail, we get right back up and keep going with absolute commitment. Clear intention gives us a certain clarity in mind. We don't ask "if" we ask "how." And when our intentions are clear, the answers about how to get the job done magically shows up. It is as if God says, "You took two steps already, you had clear intentions and determination, now I will open doors for you. I will place the right people in the right place at the right time, so that your intentions will become a reality."

"Efforting" is very costly and ultimately it won't lead you anywhere. It is born out of the fear that you are not capable or deserving. Please do not let fear stop you from being committed and from declaring your vision with crystal clear intentions. The gift of clear intentions will provide the synergy and energy to discover the right mechanism. So, by all means, keep your intentions clear.

Where do you seek wisdom or guidance? Why this person, place or thing?

How would you describe your thinking: group thinking or cutting edge thinker? What is the advantage or disadvantage to this type of thinking?

What past mistakes have you afraid of the "here and now"? What is this costing you?

In what areas of your life are you most effective?

In what areas of your life are you least effective?

What do you think is the single most awesome phenomena in the world? What is it about this thing that makes it awesome?

What in your life are you being dramatic about? ("Oh my God, I'm middle-aged; unemployed; not married.")

What in your life could you be more dramatic about? (I am smart; I am a gifted teacher, parent, coach, artist, musician, entrepreneur, etc.)

ELEVEN

Breakdown vs. Breakthrough

Whenever we find our lives (and ourselves) in a breakdown, it is actually good news! However, it does not feel good. For example, your job that used to be satisfying and fulfilling is now boring, not challenging and not quite enough to make you happy. Nevertheless, you like the steady paycheck and losing the position would really shake you up. Breakdown is always an indicator that we are committed to something bigger, and it is an opportunity to grow and stretch ourselves, instead of living life "business as usual."

Although losing your job is a breakdown and it feels like you're standing on a cliff, about to take a tumble over the edge; what a breakdown really means is that the status quo is no longer working for you. Just getting by without challenging yourself is no longer enough for you. A breakdown occurs when there is a huge gap between who you are and what you're doing with your talents.

It means your spirit is calling you forth to produce richer and more profound experiences in life. You may be living your life the same old way, but your spirit is years ahead of you. It is ready to actualize more of your potential and use more of your gifts at a higher level than you believe you are ready for.

Say yes to your all-wise, all-knowing spirit. Surrender to it and you will move forward. Have faith that on the other side of the abyss that you're staring into is the bliss that comes with breaking through your limitations. Think of a little fledgling bird that's been flapping its wings for weeks trying to leave the nest. Yes, it's comfortable there. Mommy and Daddy fly in four times a day to feed the baby bird. Yet, it longs to be free. Take an opportunity to watch through a pair of binoculars as a bird takes its first dive into the air, and you will see a look of pure freedom on its face. It is taking flight with nothing but its own wings, soaring to new heights, reaching new horizons. That is what your spirit is longing to do. To have the future that is impossible in the nest become possible in the open flight of breakthrough. The opportunity to experience your own power and abilities is waiting for you outside the nest. By all means, breakthrough and go too far so you'll know how far you can go.

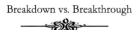

What was your last random act of kindness? What moved you to do it? How did it feel?

Name ten incompletes in your life. What would life be like if you completed these things? What is stopping you?

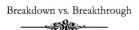

What truth are you unwilling to face about yourself or your life? What is denial costing you?

Name ten of the most unique things about you. How do you express each uniqueness?

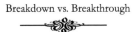

Name ten things that frighten you about life. What can you do to overcome them?

Name ten words to describe your physical body. Are you pleased with your body? What parts of your body do you need to embrace? What can't you change? What parts can you improve? Are you doing it? If not, why not?

Name ten words to describe your health. What needs to change in order to improve your health?

What was one of your most blissful moments?

What have you discovered so far?

How can these discoveries forward your life?

What actions will you have to take?

TWELVE

Spiritual Discovery

TWELVE

Having It Happen vs. How It Happens

Often, we need to give up the way we think things should look. It's better to decide that having it happen is more important than waiting until all your "ducks are in a row" or being able to present the perfect plan. Sometimes, perfection is our worst enemy because it keeps us tied up reworking and revising a plan that never seems to be finished. Whatever you have conceived of as the way it must be, I can assure you, it isn't the only way. It does not serve you or your vision to tell yourself that you won't proceed unless everything lines up with the picture you have in your mind, because life is not perfect. And what's more, you're not perfect. You can't control everything, life gets messy, chaotic, unpredictable, even with the best laid plans. If you will move ahead only when life is handing you the perfect picture, you are committed to "how it happens," not to "making it happen."

The perfect plan is always headed for a collision when it meets up with real life. People who are obsessed with perfection are obsessed with control, and control can be very limiting and tiring. Perfectionists often don't see that their own tendencies are short-circuiting their chance to succeed. This is why being a perfectionist actually ends up sabotaging your plans instead of actualizing them.

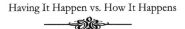

God is not going to work along with you if you don't trust life to work. You have to learn to see the wealth of possibilities available to you if you just let go and let others contribute to the plan - even though that may include flaws. You might have a great idea in your head, but however great it is, two heads are still better than one. And who knows the contribution that three or four heads could make?

Name ten things that bore you. What is it about these things? How can you use this awareness to forward your life?

Name five things that trigger you and make you angry. How can you shift your relationship with these things?

Name ten things that excite you. How much time do you spend doing these things?

Name your top three regrets?

Name an incident or time in your life when you decided you were on your own. (Who left you? Who let you down or did not support you?)

Name a time in your life when you felt you did not belong. Why did you feel this way? What was the incident? How has this impacted your sense of yourself?

Name an incident or time in your life when you were made to feel that you did not matter. Who dismissed you; minimized you or ignored your existence? How did this impact who you are today?

Name a time or incident in your life when you felt special. What decisions did you make about yourself and the world?

THIRTEEN

Living By Design vs. Letting Life Happen

The question is: Are you happening to your life or is your life happening to you? Are you living by design or are you drifting haphazardly through life, taking it as it comes? When you live by design, you take a stand that your life will count for something, that you will fulfill your soul's purpose, that you will lead with your passion, that your work will be an extension of who you are.

When you let life happen to you, you are taking life as it comes, you are letting it pass you right by. You aren't serving yourself, and you aren't serving anyone else. If you look at your experience, you will see that your passion is missing, and your purpose is going unfulfilled. When you meet a person who is living his/her purpose, you will find someone who is full of passion, completely engaged, and intoxicated with their life. So go ahead, get in the driver's seat of your life and live your life by your design. Become intoxicated with your dreams. Fall in love with your passion. Surrender to your purpose. I challenge you to happen to your life. Don't let life happen to you. You won't regret it. In fact, you will be elated.

What or who in your life do you need to have closure with? What would open up for you as a result of closure?

What is between you and your biggest goal? What do you need to do to remove this obstacle? (Both internal and external.)

Describe your first heartbreak. Who broke your heart? What conclusions did you come to about love because of it?

Who has disappointed you the most? How is this disappointment impacting you now?

If you could live your life over, what would you change? Why?

What life lesson have you refused to learn? (Notice repeated patterns or themes.) What is this costing you?

Who has hurt you the most? (Describe the experience in detail; the incident, your feelings, words exchanged, physical impact, emotional scars, etc.) What did you learn from this experience? How can you use this learning to forward your life?

Who has been the biggest surprise to you, positive or negative? (A child's success, spouse's love/infidelity, colleague's support/deceit, friends' jealousy/joy.)

FOURTEEN

Your Past Does Not Equal Your Future

If you decide today that your past will not determine your future, then it won't. Unfortunately, most people drag their past with them wherever they go, letting their previous mistakes, relationships, failures, and heartbreaks limit and shape what they are capable of doing and being. You have the power to shape your own future through your visions, your dreams, and your desires. Usually, people react to the past and make decisions based on what they don't want to happen. For example, "My last boyfriend was x-y-z, so I don't want that again. I'll avoid anyone who even looks like he might be that way." Most people live their lives in reaction to the past; making sure that their past does not happen again, as opposed to creating from their heartfelt desires and what matters to them in the present.

Right now, in this very moment, your future is a blank canvas waiting for you to paint a picture. What do you want to paint? What are your dreams and passions? Why would you want to just paint your history? Once we accept our life as a blank canvas and that we are not our past, the possibilities are limitless. But if we look into our future using the past as our guide, we run a huge risk of creating more of the same. The same frustration, the same failures, the same mistakes, the same problems. Which do you prefer, more of the same or a brand new picture filled with endless possibilities?

Are you most comfortable giving or receiving? What does this say about you?

What are you pretending not to know? What emotions and truths are you stuffing out of sight and out of mind? What are the consequences of these actions?

What are you trying to prove to yourself and others?

?

Who do you need to forgive? What is not forgiving this person costing you?

What do you need to forgive in yourself? What is not forgiving yourself costing you?

What friend do you enjoy the most? What is it about this person that brings you joy?

Who have you not loved unconditionally and how has this impacted your life?

What do you love most about your family?

FIFTEEN

Psychological Assessment vs. Committed Action

What is the difference between psychological assessment and committed action? The difference is "analysis paralysis", staying stuck and recreating the *"same- old same- old"*, rather than discovering, learning, and moving forward. Psychological assessment is centered in a victimized, whiny, me-focused context. It is when we look at life through the lens of critic, judge, or detractor. We view things from the paradigm, right versus wrong, good or bad, like or don't like, agree or disagree. None of these perspectives will provide new insight, neither will they open new possibilities, and they absolutely will not demand anything new of you. They don't shed any new light on the situation. In fact, these perspectives just keep rehashing old information.

When we examine situations from a place of discovery and ask ourselves committed action questions, we look to see what is working, what is not working, and what can we do differently. These three simple questions will provide access to parts of ourselves that will never be available in psychological assessment. So, it is imperative that we challenge ourselves and look beyond what we already know and ask, "What is it that I don't know that would open new possibilities, lend itself to new horizons, and create the extraordinary?" It is with this new awarenes that we are able to challenge ourselves and take new actions to create different results.

What do you love most about yourself? Why?

What do you think is the greatest gift a parent could give their child?

Whose life have you personally impacted in a positive way? What difference did it make?

Name three positive characteristics about your mother. How did these things shape your life? Why?

Name three negative characteristics about your mother. How did these things shape your life? Why?

Name three positive characteristics about your father. How did these things shape your life? Why?

Name three negative characteristics about your father. How did these things shape your life? Why?

Who is a courageous person that you admire? What is courageous about this person?

SIXTEEN

Scarcity vs. Abundance

Scarcity, put simply, is a fear-based mentality. It is the belief that there will never be enough. If you go around thinking, "Oh my God, I better not use the best china, I might break it," you probably suffer from this affliction. Or, "Even though I'm miserable at my job, I better hang onto it because I'll never find another one." Sound familiar?

Scarcity assumes the worst. It is a limiting belief and causes us to shrink in response to new opportunities. If you believe the world won't come through for you, then every step into the unknown will feel like a risk. Worse, a scarcity mentality results in a profound stinginess of spirit. We are afraid to give of our time, money, and love because of the recurring thought, "What if I run out?" This mentality reduces us to living in a cave – it is that restrictive. You might save and save and keep every penny you make, but you never feel rich or expansive. You're too busy trying not to lose.

My childhood was filled with abundance, even though our family income wavered. There was always plenty of love and good will, and this kept us happy. My childhood gave me the knowledge that the world is abundant if you look at it that way. Too often, we confuse accumulation with abundance. Many of us have lots of things, but we don't have abundant consciousness because we have a stingy spirit. Becoming full of abundance is your birthright. All you have to do is open yourself to the blessings of the world.

Describe your sexual life. What and who impacted this part of you the most?

Who or what brings you immense joy? How often do you spend time with these people or doing these things?

If you could change one thing about your mate, what would you change?

Who was your first love? How did this love shape your view of relationships and love?

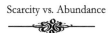

How do you show up for the world? How would the world describe you? (Friends, Family, or Colleagues?) Describe each point of view separately.

When you were growing up what was your favorite childhood game? What does this imply about your character or makeup?

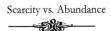

What do you trust most about your children?

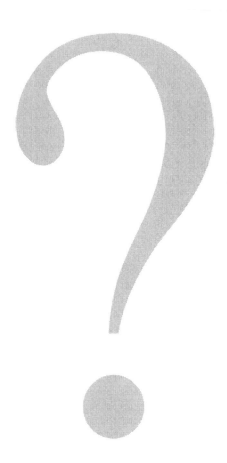

What do you trust least about your children?

SEVENTEEN

Spirituality

The words religion and spirituality are used interchangeably, but they really aren't the same thing. Religion is a system of beliefs that tends to be steeped in dogma. We are told what to believe by some authority figure, and all too often, the convictions they pass on are limiting and harsh. The people who accept them are judgmental, especially towards those who don't share the same beliefs. Read the newspapers. They are filled with stories about people who attack others for not having the same religious beliefs.

On the other hand, spirituality is the understanding that we do not own our bodies. They're just on loan. We are really made up of spirit. In the last twenty years or so, there has been a lot of talk about the authentic self, which to me is really the God-self. It is the spirit we came to the planet with at birth. We are never more in touch with our immaculately spiritual side than when we are babies. What do you see when you look into a baby's eyes? Their eyes radiate light. Quite simply, they are pure spirit. They are free with their expression of wonder and they find magic everywhere they look. If they find wonder everywhere, you might ask yourself if they would even know a miracle when they see one. What if they saw a ball falling upward? Yes, they would think it was a miracle. But they also think that a ball falling downward is a miracle too, and who is to say that it isn't? The only reason adults don't see it that way is that we are used to the miracles of everyday life

Do you remember how fully alive you felt as a small child? All the things we take for granted – like breathing, walking and talking – are interesting, sensual experiences for a child. And they are completely honest about their emotions. When they're happy, they are unabashedly happy and they show it. When they're unhappy, they burst into tears. Children don't know how to be duplicitous. In other words, they are their own authentic selves.

And then they begin to develop. They have experiences, learn a language, try to fit in with their family circle, and find a way to become useful in this world. Life starts to happen. When you are a baby, everything is a "YES." Your mother magically seems to know when you're hungry or sleepy or need your diapers changed. You don't know how she knows. All you're doing is letting out a yell. She can read your mind and she will fall all over herself to tend to your every need.

As you grow up though, the powerful word NO begins to reveal itself. There are a lot of limits in this world, and children hear about them from everyone they meet. "Don't run into the street." "Don't talk in class." "Don't touch the merchandise." "NO" makes you begin to disconnect from your spirit, your authentic self, because you become covered in the clutter of disappointment. You forget who you are on an essential level. You stop radiating light and start believing that those disappointments are who you really are. You don't see that they are merely the events that happened to you.

You forget that spirit is your own essence and that you are, indeed, the spirit of God.

What do you like the most about your significant other? What does this reflect about you?

Who and what motivates you?

What race of people outside of your race are you comfortable with? Why this race? What influenced this decision? How can you use this awareness to broaden your relationships?

What is the ideal you? How is this person different from who you are now?

What do you say to yourself when you let yourself down in a big way? Are you understanding and compassionate or abusive and judgmental? Are your words empowering you to do better next time or are they discouraging?

When you are faced with a challenge, do you determine your own course or do you let circumstances determine it for you? In other words, who is in the driver's seat?

How often do you affirm your vision of what you are committed to achieving?

In your world view, is the cup half-empty or is it half-full? (Notice how your view is reflected in your language.)

EIGHTEEN

Victim Mentality vs. Responsibility

When we relate to circumstances from a responsible approach, we are empowering ourselves to move through the world with strength and conviction. It is hard for some people to understand this concept. "How can I take responsibility for what happens to me? I don't control the world." No, you don't. You cannot control events; what you can control, however, is your reaction to events.

The world is a big and chaotic place, and anything can happen, including disaster, disappointment, and heartbreak, so you are bound to get a few bumps and bruises once in a while. This is true for everyone. This is just the way life is. So, what does this realistic approach mean to you? When something happens to you, you can decide whether to be a victim or whether to act from a place of power. You face a crucial choice when adversity strikes. Are you going to say, "Poor me" or "Why is the world doing this to me?" The truth is that the world isn't doing anything to you; it's just doing what it's doing. You just happened to be at that spot at that time. If it's another person who is the source of your unhappiness, it's just people being people. How the universe works is neutral. If you take it personally, it drains your power by putting you in the position of a victim.

People who react with self-pity are beaten down by events.

People who respond by taking responsibility can actually use their misfortune to make a difference. MADD – Mothers Against Drunk Drivers – was started by a woman in anguish because her child was killed by a drunk driver who had had several prior arrests for driving while intoxicated. Out of her grief, she made the decision that no other mother should have to go through what she did, and she started lobbying Congress for tougher legislation. She couldn't bring her child back, but she could use the experience and the pain to help others.

One other thing we can see from this example is that taking responsibility not only changes what we do in the world, but who we are in the world. The responsible person experiences themselves as strong and capable because they operate from a place of choice. "Okay, I can't change what happened, but I can keep it from destroying me. I can determine to learn from this and create a bigger platform from which to live." Contrast this with the victim perspective of no choice, no power, and hyper-reactivity. When life is happening TO you, you see yourself as a sacrificial lamb headed to the slaughter. You feel vulnerable all the time, which makes you reactive to the tiniest slight from others. Out of pure defensiveness, you become overly self-protective, always assuming ill-intent where there is none. Our approach to what happens to us really matters. It determines the very essence of our quality of life. So while we cannot always choose what happens nor always control what happens to us, we always, always, have a choice about how we relate to what happens, whether from the responsible context, meaning the power and ability to choose how you will relate to what has happened, or the victim context meaning blaming others and giving over all of our power to something or someone outside of ourselves. The power of choice! Everything we do is a choice, every way that we are is a choice, and even choosing not to choose is a choice. The choice is yours: victim or responsible; disempowered and weak or powerful and empowered, for that is the difference between the two. I vote responsible! What do you choose?

What dream do you desire, that you are unconsciously waiting for someone to say it's okay to have? Why are you waiting for permission?

What part of yourself have you lost that would be a joy to recover?

Name ten things that you think you should do differently in your life. Why?

Name ten things you should continue to do in your life. Why?

Describe a time when you were most exhilarated. What were you doing?

Describe a time when you were most out of your comfort zone. What was it about this event that made you "stretch"? And what did you learn?

If you were going to write a book, what would it be about? Why?

Describe the wisdom of your mother or her lack of wisdom. How has this impacted your wisdom?

NINETEEN

Reasons or Results

At the end of the road called life, you will either have one or the other: A reason or a story about why life did not turn out, or you will have a full life with extraordinary results. The prize isn't the number of years you've spent on earth. The real prize is the quality of life – how many dreams you fulfilled, how many promises you kept, what visions you brought to reality.

If, looking back, we see that we constantly gave in to our stories, excuses and justifications, we will understand that we took power away from our vision. It is similar to driving a car where air constantly seeps out of the tires. We are living with a slow leak. Eventually, our car rumbles along, the ride becomes bumpy and uncomfortable. When excuses become the ride of life, it loses its vitality, its joy and its meaning. And before we know it, our car and our lives are parked on the side of the road.

Look around at the elders in your life. Look at their faces. It will be evident what kind of choices they made along the way. Their faces and eyes will be filled with joy, wisdom, and a powerful resolve, or their eyes will be filled with regret, remiss, and disappointment. Eventually, life always shows up on our faces. At the end of this journey called life, we will either be bitter, depressed or defeated, or alive, fulfilled and joyful. The good news is that we have a choice in the matter! WE can choose to give power to our reasons, stories, and excuses or we can choose to give power to the fact that our life is a gift, dreams are blessings, and visions are sacred. We as human beings will always, always, be right without exception. So what will you be right about? Will it be your stories, excuses and justifications, or the blessing and sacredness that life is? The choice is yours! Reasons or results, which will it be?

Name ten things that you would like to be different in your life. What actions are you willing to take?

What in life do you feel unworthy of? (For example: love, joy, prosperity, fantastic life, etc.) (Stop, think, NOW answer.)

What inner voice or message have you been ignoring? (it's like a nag) Why?

What is the one thing about yourself that you most want to change? Why?

What ongoing thoughts shape your reality?

What are you passionate about?

What components in your life do you need in order to find perfect peace?

Are you aging gracefully or are you aging prematurely? What is the contributor to this process?

TWENTY

Certainty in Times of Uncertainty

There will be times in life when we are not sure how we accomplish a goal or a task. For the faint of heart or for the very careful, this will make it very difficult to take the first step. It is not important that we know exactly how, it is only important that in these times of uncertainty, with or without a clear-cut path or a guarantee, that we operate from a place of certainty and have clarity of faith and a strong sense of determination. These attributes will be the determining factor in the end. Not how much we knew at the onset, but our willingness to go the distance and stay the path when we were unsure. When we learn this lesson and we're willing to embrace this as human beings, as the old cliché says, "the sky is the limit." In fact there is no limit!

When we are willing to continue with faith and determination and remain certain even when we are uncertain of the "how", we shall accomplish and prevail in all things. In fact, this distinction of life is the key that unlocks the internal obstacles that so frequently deter us when clarity and certainty is not yet available. So, I invite you to pick up the key of certainty and be sure and unlock the doors in times of uncertainty.

What do you think happens to the human spirit and soul when you mak the final transition? How does this impact the way you live your life?

Describe the wisdom of God? How can you use this wisdom to live a more empowered life?

Name the top twenty things you want to do before you die.

Describe the difference between spirituality and religion. How has this belief impacted the way you live?

What would you do if you knew it was your last birthday?

What forces in nature do you feel most connected to? The river, the ocean, the trees? How do these forces take you out of your self-centered world?

What would you do if you were better organized? What is being disorganized costing you?

TWENTY-ONE

Tell the Truth

The truth will set you free. Famous words, but how many of us really understand them? There really is value in the old saying that you have to be able to look yourself in the mirror and like what you see. The problem is that the truth usually scares us. It reveals facts that mean we have to make a change or take a risk or sacrifice something. Whatever it reveals is powerful! Sometimes the truth pisses us off. It reveals a fact about us that we don't want to acknowledge. However, the moment we tell the truth about something, we begin to own it. As a famous psychologist says, "You can't change what you don't own." Once we own it, we can begin to have the power to change it. If we don't own it, then it has the power over us. The secrets in life, which we keep behind closed curtains, haunt us and influence us in ways we cannot control. They bring up guilt, shame, and the fear of being found out. Pretending not to know, ignoring, and brushing things under the carpet does not make it not so.

If I am afraid of looking at something but I face up to it anyway and acknowledge that I am afraid, in that moment I have power over that fear instead of it having power over me. This means that I have the capacity to overcome my fears simply by facing them. Until I tell the truth about it though, there is no chance that I can move beyond the issue. So tell the truth and experience the freedom and the power available to you when you tell it like it is.

When you look into a child's eyes, what do you see?

How can you serve the world? Are you doing it?

What truly inspires you?

What is the greatest thing about being a human being?

?

In what areas of your life have you been a leader? How did or does it feel?

?

In what area of your life have you been a follower? How did it work?

What parts of your life do you have yet to master?

If you were to have a breakthrough in your life, what area would you want it to be in? What would you create and how would you experience yourself differently?

Name ten blessings you are grateful for.

To book Sylvia High for speaking engagements, trainings or life coaching please contact her directly at Aiming High Incorporated 925 634-0755 or at aiminghighinc@hotmail.com

29930879R00129

Made in the USA
San Bernardino, CA
01 February 2016